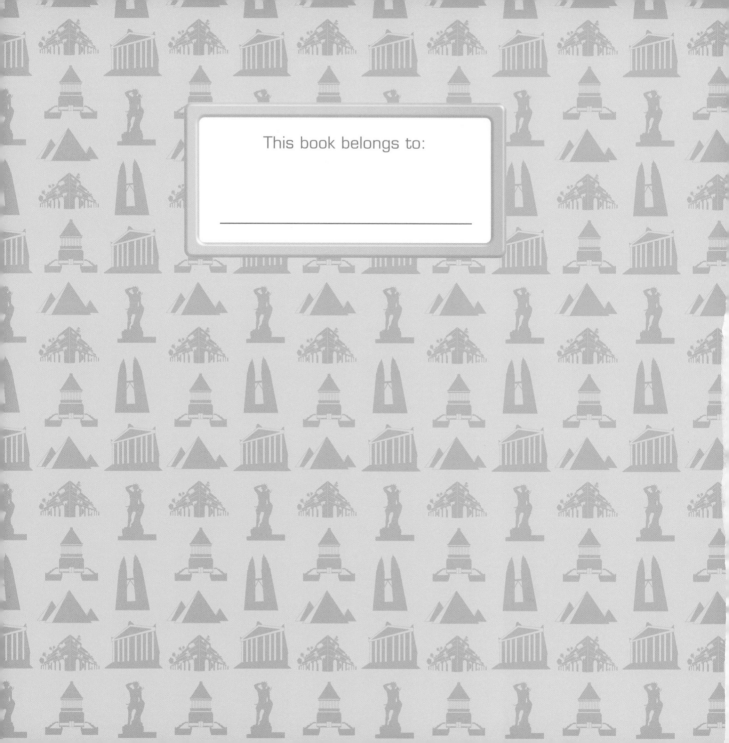

This book belongs to:

_____

Wonders
of the World

© 2010 Top That! Publishing plc
This 2011 edition published by Sandy Creek, by arrangement with Top That! Publishing plc

Sandy Creek
122 Fifth Avenue, New York, NY 10011
ISBN-13: 978-1-4351-3200-9
Printed and bound in Guangdong, China
Manufactured April 2011
Lot 1 3 5 7 9 10 8 6 4 2

CONTENTS

2

CONTENTS

THE PYRAMIDS OF GIZA

The Great Pyramid of Khufu, or Cheops, was the tallest structure on Earth for 43 centuries. It is both the oldest and the best preserved wonder of the ancient world.

What are the pyramids of Giza

The pyramids contain the tombs of ancient Egyptian kings or pharaohs. There are three large pyramids at Giza, a "necropolis" or city of the dead, outside Cairo. The largest and oldest is the Great Pyramid of Khufu, or Cheops, which was once 481 ft (145.75 m) high. Nearby are the Pyramids of Khefre and Menkaure and the famous Sphinx statue.

Pyramids are found in Egypt

Slaves hauling large stone blocks

How was the Great Pyramid built

The Great Pyramid took twenty years to build during Pharaoh Khufu's reign, around 2560 BC. Thousands of slaves carved and carried two million stone blocks, each weighing over 2 tons (1,814 kg). Ramps were used to drag the blocks into place. The pyramid was covered in smooth stone—bits of which can still be seen near the top of Khefre's pyramid.

What is the significance of the shape of the pyramids

The pyramids have a very geometrical shape. The ancient Egyptians thought that using fixed shapes like the square, the circle and the triangle in their buildings would allow their civilization to survive floods and droughts. They thought that the shape of the pyramid, reaching out to the stars, would bring the pharaoh closer to the gods and make him live forever.

The Great Pyramid at Giza

King's burial chamber

Queen's chamber

Grand gallery

Queen's passage

Unfinished chamber

What is the Sphinx ?

The magical statue of the Sphinx at Giza has a lion's body and the face of Pharaoh Khefre. It is 241 ft (73.5 m) long and 65 ft (20 m) high. The Sphinx was carved out of solid rock around the time of the construction of the Pyramid of Khefre in 2555–2532 BC.

The Sphinx at Giza

What is inside the Great Pyramid ?

Mysterious corridors and galleries lead to Khufu's burial chamber at the heart of the pyramid. The pyramid was so well designed that there is only one third of an inch (1 cm) between the tomb and the chamber walls. The galleries once contained beautiful precious objects, but robbers have stolen everything. Khufu's servants may have been sacrificed inside the pyramid.

THE STATUE OF ZEUS AT OLYMPIA

To bring the god of thunderbolts to life and celebrate the Olympic Games, the most famous ancient Greek sculptor created an enormous golden statue.

What were the ancient Olympic Games ?

In Greek legend, gods and goddesses came from a mountain outside Olympia, 43 miles (70 km) from Athens. Every year from 776 BC to AD 391, wars stopped all over the Greek world and athletes came to Olympia for competitive games in honor of Zeus, "the father of gods and men".

GREECE

• Athens

The ancient Olympic Games were held near Athens

Entrance to the original Olympic stadium, Olympia

The impressive Statue of Zeus at Olympia

Who was Zeus

Zeus lived on mountain tops and in clouds, where he kept an eye on the other Olympian gods and naughty humans, too. Although he was the most important god, Zeus often had to zap other Olympians with thunderbolts to keep them in order. The Olympians were definitely not "one big, happy family": Zeus's father Kronos ate his own children!

When was the Statue of Zeus built

In 430 BC, the sculptor Pheidias finished a terrifying 42-ft (13-m) statue. The height of a four-story building, the statue barely fitted into the Temple of Zeus. Visitors had the statue's feet at eye level. Zeus was seated but looked as though he was about to explode out of the temple. His flesh was ivory, his drapery gold, and his throne was decorated with precious stones.

What happened to the Statue of Zeus

The Olympic Games were outlawed in AD 391 by the Christian Emperor Theodosius I. The temple was closed and then badly damaged by earthquakes, landslides and floods. In the fifth century AD, the ruined statue was taken to a palace in Constantinople, where it was unfortunately destroyed by fire in AD 462.

How was the Statue built

Pheidias built a wooden frame on which sheets of metal and ivory were placed. He sculpted and carved the different pieces of the statue in a workshop before assembling them in the temple. As the statue was designed to be out of proportion to the temple, it looked bigger than it was. For almost four hundred years, it fascinated everyone who saw it.

FACT FILE

Pheidias also made the marble sculptures on the Parthenon in Athens. These are known as the Elgin Marbles and can today be seen in the British Museum in London.

FACT FILE

The Statue of Zeus held a figure of the winged goddess of victory in one hand. Her name was Nike, which is where the sports brand name comes from!

The ruined Temple of Zeus

THE HANGING GARDENS OF BABYLON

The massive walled city of Babylon was full of wonders, but none could match the Hanging Gardens, the greatest example of hydraulic engineering in the ancient world.

Where was Babylon ?

Babylon was built on the banks of the River Euphrates in Iraq. This area is called "the cradle of civilization", because the world's first cities were constructed there. Babylon had massive walls, one hundred bronze gates and brightly tiled buildings full of golden statues of the god Marduk. The 300-ft (91-m), multi-colored Tower of Babel stood at the city's heart.

Babylon, on the River Euphrates

Who built the Hanging Gardens ?

In 570 BC, King Nebuchadnezzar II built an enormous terraced garden next to his palace, to please his wife Amyitis. Nebuchadnezzar was a great military commander, and was very proud of making Babylon the most beautiful city in the world. Bricks in Babylon bore the inscription "Nebuchadnezzar made this".

King Nebuchadnezzar

Why were the Hanging Gardens so special ?

The Hanging Gardens were built on an 80-ft (24-m) high, man-made hill. The hilltop was packed with beautiful and exotic trees and flowers. The hill was actually a series of terraces—also full of flowers and plants—supported by strong pillars. Ingenious machines called chain pumps helped to irrigate the garden. Although the gardens didn't really "hang" the name probably came from a Greek word meaning "overhanging" and they must have been an impressive sight with their beautiful plants overhanging terraces and arches.

The beautiful Hanging Gardens at Babylon

Why might the Hanging Gardens be a myth

As Babylonian records make no mention of the Hanging Gardens, they may have been a myth. However, archaeologists have discovered possible evidence of garden cellars and chain pumps. The River Euphrates would have provided the water needed for the plants which would have been transported in buckets on the chain pump.

The Hanging Gardens were irrigated with water from the River Euphrates

How did chain pumps work ?

Two wheels, one above the other, were connected by a chain, on which buckets were hung. When slaves turned the lower wheel, the buckets dipped into the River Euphrates and picked up water. The chain then lifted the buckets to the upper wheel, where they fed water channels running down through the Gardens.

The chain pump mechanism

What happened to the Gardens ?

The Hanging Gardens were first described when the warrior-king Alexander the Great invaded in 331 BC. By the time of the Persian invasion in the second century BC, the Hanging Gardens had disappeared, along with the city of Babylon.

Alexander the Great

FACT FILE

Babylon got all its food from the nearby Plain of Edin, which is the Bible's Garden of Eden

THE TEMPLE OF ARTEMIS

Antipater of Sidon, the man who listed the Seven Wonders of the World in the second century BC, thought that this was the best of them all!

Why was the Temple so impressive ❓

The Temple of Artemis at Ephesus—on Turkey's Mediterranean coast—was built in about 550 BC. It was enormous and made out of marble. The Temple was 260 ft (80 m) wide, 420 ft (130 m) long and had 127 60-ft (18-m) high columns. The overall height of the Temple was 80 ft (24 m). The Temple housed four huge bronze statues of warrior women, or Amazons.

The ruins of the Temple of Artemis

Who was Artemis ❓

Artemis was the Greek goddess of hunting and fertility. According to legend, she was friendly to humans, especially children, and also protected animals. At night, she was supposed to dance through the countryside, firing arrows of moonlight from a silver bow. Artemis was still very popular in the early days of Christianity.

Statue of the Greek goddess Artemis

The Temple of Artemis is at Ephesus

Who was Herostratus

In 356 BC, a man in Ephesus called Herostratus was obsessed with becoming famous. He burned down the Temple of Artemis so that everyone would talk about him, but the authorities made it illegal to say his name! The Temple burned down on the night that Alexander the Great was born. Legend says that Artemis was too busy at the birth to save her own temple.

Why did the Temple become an important Christian site

St Paul preached in the Temple in the first century AD and was almost attacked by the angry worshippers of Artemis. Legend has it that the Virgin Mary, accompanied by St Paul, came to Ephesus at the end of her life, sometime between AD 37 and AD 45. St John is said to have lived the last years of his life nearby.

Statue of the Virgin Mary

When was the Temple rebuilt

When Alexander the Great conquered Asia Minor, he helped rebuild the Temple, which was finished by 335 BC. In AD 262, Goths destroyed the Temple, but Artemis was still so popular that the Ephesians vowed to rebuild it. For some reason, they never did.

Why are there only seven wonders of the ancient world

In ancient times, the number seven was thought to be the purest of numbers—which is why Antipater of Sidon included only seven wonders on his list!

Marble statues, Ephesus Museum, Seljuk, Turkey

FACT FILE

Some of the remains of the Temple of Artemis can be seen in the Ephesus Museum, Turkey and the British Museum, London.

The Temple of Artemis

THE MAUSOLEUM OF HALICARNASSUS

The world's first great memorial monument was packed with statues of lions, horses and people—all the things that Satrap Mausolus loved in life.

What does the word "mausoleum" mean

The word "mausoleum" means a large, stately tomb. The history of the word dates back to 350 BC, when a magnificent tomb was built for Mausolus, the ruler of Halicarnassus, a large port on the Aegean Sea in south-west Turkey. Mausolus's "mausoleum" was planned by his wife, Artemisia.

The port of Halicarnassus is now known as Bodrum

What is a satrap

Mausolus was a satrap, or local governor, for the mighty Persian Empire. In the century before the Mausoleum was built, the Persian Empire spread from Iran into Iraq, Northern India, Syria, Egypt and Turkey. The empire was so big, local rulers were used to help control people.

A figure of Mausolus

Mausolus's province of Caria was almost 1,000 miles (1,600 km) from the Persian capital of Persepolis.

Who were the Amazons

The Mausoleum of Halicarnassus was decorated with a frieze depicting fighting Amazons—bits can be seen today in the British Museum in London. In legend, the Amazons were warrior women who fought Greek heroes. The Amazon queens Hippolyte, Penthesilea and Antiope were very strong

The ornate frieze depicting fighting Amazons

and very beautiful. Female societies really did exist in Ukraine and Libya—and evidence suggests that they were great horsewomen and fearless fighters.

Why were there so many statues on the Mausoleum

The 140-ft (45-m) Mausoleum was famous for its statues of people and animals. The tomb stood on a podium covered with statues—the roof was teeming with them and a huge statue of a chariot pulled by four horses adorned the top. It was the first ancient building dedicated to the memory of a human being rather than a god.

The remains of a colossal horse from the quadriga of the Mausoleum at Halicarnassus

Why was the Mausoleum destroyed

In AD 1494, Crusader soldiers called the Knights of St John of Malta decided to fortify a nearby castle with stones from the Mausoleum. By AD 1522, the whole Mausoleum had been taken to pieces and used. The massive Crusader castle still stands at Bodrum, and the polished stone and marble blocks from the Mausoleum can be seen within the walls.

Crusader castle at Bodrum

FACT FILE

The proper word for a stone tomb is a "sarcophagus", which is ancient Greek for "flesh eater"!

You can still see the foundations of the Mausoleum if you visit Bodrum in Turkey.

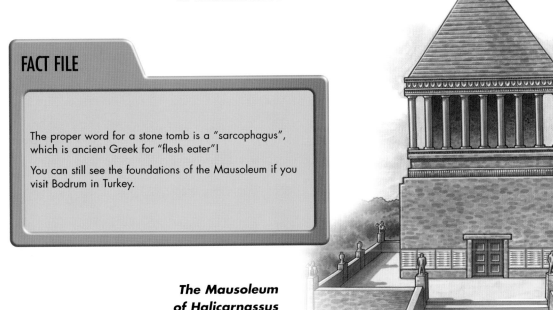

The Mausoleum of Halicarnassus

THE COLOSSUS OF RHODES

This enormous, polished bronze statue shone like the sun for only 56 years, but it became a powerful symbol of unity for all Greek people.

Why was the Colossus built

Ancient Greece was made up of city-states that often fought each other. On the island of Rhodes there were three such states, but, in 408 BC, they united. One hundred years later, to celebrate a unity that was now the envy of all Greece, the people of Rhodes built an enormous statue to their sun god, Helios. The Colossus was finished in 282 BC.

The Greek island of Rhodes housed the Colossus

Where did the Colossus stand ?

For a long time it was thought that the Colossus straddled the mouth of the main harbor in Rhodes, but, given the great height of the statue and the width of the harbor mouth, this is impossible. Recent research suggests that the Colossus was actually erected on the eastern side of the harbor.

How was the Colossus constructed ?

The bronze skin was made in pieces in the workshop of a local sculptor, Chares. The feet and ankles were fixed to a white marble base and the skin slowly attached to an iron and stone frame. An earth ramp was used to work on the top. When the Colossus was finished, it was 110 ft (33 m) high.

The iron and stone frame of the Colossus

How was the statue paid for ?

Rhodes traded a lot with Egypt. In 305 BC, King Seleucus I of Macedonia besieged the island in an attempt to break this trade link between Rhodes and his enemy, Ptolemy I of Egypt. Seleucus's army eventually sailed away, leaving behind their military equipment. The people of Rhodes sold this and used the money to build the Colossus.

When was the Colossus destroyed ?

The statue stood at the harbor entrance until an earthquake in 226 BC broke its knees and the Colossus fell over. The Egyptians offered to restore the statue, but an oracle forbade it. For nearly 900 years the Colossus lay in ruins, until AD 654, when the remains were sold to a Syrian merchant. Nine hundred camels were used to take the fragments away!

The statue destroyed

THE LIGHTHOUSE OF ALEXANDRIA

Sailors appreciated this lighthouse because it protected them. Builders stood in awe because it was then the tallest structure on Earth. Scientists wondered how the mysterious mirror worked!

Where was Alexandria

Alexander the Great built an empire stretching from Greece to Persia, Egypt and Asia Minor. He founded a city in Egypt, on the Mediterranean coast, and called it Alexandria. After his death in 323 BC, the empire split. Ptolemy I assumed power in Egypt and made Alexandria the greatest city in the world. Seleucos I of Macedonia ruled the empire from Greece to Babylon.

The city of Alexandria is in Egypt

Who built the Lighthouse of Alexandria

The building of the Lighthouse on Pharos, an island in Alexandria's harbor, took twenty years and was completed in 270 BC. The finest scientists, mathematicians and artists of the age planned the structure and its mirror in the famous Alexandria Library. The Lighthouse was 384 ft (117 m) high—the equivalent of a modern-day, 40-story building.

Why did Alexandria need a lighthouse

Alexandria was the greatest port on the Mediterranean Sea, but its double harbor made sailing dangerous. Luckily, the coastline around Alexandria was very flat so building a lighthouse to warn ships was not difficult. When the Lighthouse was completed, it was the tallest building on Earth!

How bright was the light reflected from the Lighthouse

According to historians, the huge mirror at the top of the Lighthouse was so well made, the light it reflected could be seen 35 miles (50 km) away. Apparently, the reflection was so intense it could burn up enemy ships! The mirror reflected sunlight during the day and a fire set in front of it at night. It was probably lifted into place using the internal shaft of the structure, which was also used to lift the fuel for the fire.

The intense light reflected from the Lighthouse

What happened to the Lighthouse

The Lighthouse of Alexandria remained in use for almost fourteen centuries, until it was damaged by earthquakes in AD 1303 and AD 1323. The Egyptian Sultan, Qaitbay, used blocks from the Lighthouse to build a massive fortification in AD 1480. Recently, divers discovered the remains of the Lighthouse in the harbor at Alexandria.

The harbor at Alexandria today

FACT FILE

The Lighthouse of Alexandria was so famous, it still appeared on Roman coins hundreds of years after it was built.

The Lighthouse of Alexandria

THE GRAND CANYON

Discover how the most spectacular canyon in the world was made—and how you could be walking on the bottom of an ancient sea bed if you go there!

How big is the Grand Canyon ?

The awesome Grand Canyon cuts through the Colorado Plateau in Arizona. It is 290 miles (466 km) long, 10 miles (16 km) wide and 1 mile (1.6 km) deep. The Colorado River runs through the Canyon, roaring over 200 rapids and dropping 2,200 ft (670 m) as it makes its way to the Gulf of California.

Grand Canyon

Colorado Plateau

ARIZONA

The Grand Canyon cuts through the Colorado Plateau in Arizona

How was the Grand Canyon made ?

The Grand Canyon is the most spectacular example of "erosion" in the world. The Colorado Plateau was created by violent movements on Earth's surface two billion years ago. The Grand Canyon has been carved by the movement of the Colorado River over this plateau during the last six million years.

The eroded rocks that form the Grand Canyon

Aerial view of the Colorado River

The craggy and rocky terrain of the Grand Canyon

Why are there fossils at the top of the canyon

Visitors to the top of the canyon are walking on the bottom of an ancient sea bed—that is why you can find fossils there! Five hundred million years ago, the whole plateau was under water. When sea creatures died, the minerals in the sea turned them into fossils. Then the plateau was pushed out of the sea by massive explosions.

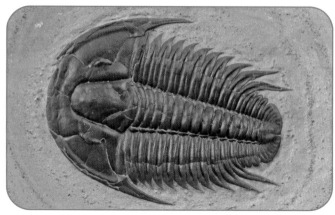

A fossilized trilobite

Why has the Grand Canyon changed in recent years

Over 2,000 species used to live in the Canyon. The ecology of the area depends on floods, but a dam, opened in 1963, now regulates the river. The damage caused by floods has been immense—much more than that caused by five million tourists every year and pollution from nearby cities and power plants.

An aerial view of the Grand Canyon

Who discovered the Grand Canyon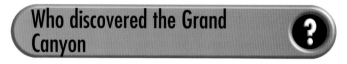

The first European to see the Canyon was a Spanish conquistador, Garcia Lopez de Cardenas in 1540. From the top, the river was so far away that he mistook it for a stream—and then wondered why it took three days to get there!
In 1869, American John Wesley Powell took a boat down the entire length of the Canyon—a dangerous trip that took three months.

John Wesley Powell

THE NORTHERN LIGHTS

At the northern reaches of our planet, the raging sun and Earth's magnetic fields create the ultimate light show!

The Northern Lights, or aurora borealis, form a 2,000-mile (3,218-km) wide oval above the Earth's magnetic north pole. At night, the Lights start as a faint glow on the horizon. Slowly, they turn into an astonishing green, red, pink, blue and violet curtain of light that curves and bends across the sky.

The stunning sight of the "aurora borealis"

The Southern Lights, or aurora australis, occur over Earth's Southern Hemisphere. The Southern and Northern Lights are connected by Earth's magnetic field. Their displays are symmetrical, which means that the shape of the Northern Lights is a mirror image of the Southern Lights. The planets Saturn, Jupiter and Uranus also have colorful auroras over their magnetic poles.

Auroras occur at the Poles

How are auroras caused

Auroras are caused by the sun, which shoots a stream of matter and energy into space. When this stream, called a solar wind, reaches Earth it smashes into Earth's magnetic field. Particles from the stream spiral

Solar winds

down towards Earth's magnetic poles. When they encounter Earth's atmosphere, these particles react with oxygen and nitrogen to make colorful swirls in the sky.

Where do you go to see an aurora

In the Northern Hemisphere, the best place to see auroras is outside Fairbanks in Alaska. In the Southern Hemisphere, the best place is off the coast of Antarctica. During violent solar winds, Earth's magnetic poles shift. Then the aurora slips towards the equator, giving sky-gazers as far south as Mexico a real treat!

The coast of Antarctica is the best place to see auroras in the Southern Hemisphere

What did ancient peoples think the lights were

In Scandinavia, where the lights are really spectacular, people thought they were dragons battling in the sky. Inuits believed that the lights were torches held by the dead, showing the dying how to get to heaven. More recently, the lights were thought to be reflections of the dawn, the sun or the moon on ice in the atmosphere.

Inuits believed that the lights were torches held by the dead

FACT FILE

Earth is like a huge magnet that is surrounded by a magnetic field that can attract or repel things. Earth also has "poles", or places where its magnetic power is concentrated.

THE VOLCANO OF PARICUTIN

There are active volcanoes all over the world, but only once have people seen a terrifying volcano born right in front of them.

Who saw the Volcano first ?

On 20th February, 1943, a farmer named Dionisio Pulido was working on his land in Paricutin, a Mexican village. Suddenly, the ground opened up and a cone of earth rose with a thunderous noise, spewing out hot ash. Within a day, the cone had grown 150 ft (45 m) and was shooting rocks 1,000 ft (304 m) into the air.

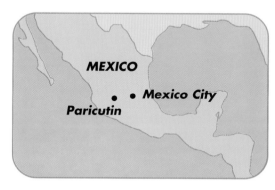

Paricutin in Mexico—site of the volcano

How much damage did the Volcano of Paricutin do ?

Molten matter called "lava" poured out of the volcano and swallowed up two villages—you can still see the church spires sticking out of the lava field. The lava flowed for nine years, eventually covering 10 sq miles (25 sq km). Luckily, only three people died—they were struck by lightning caused by the eruption.

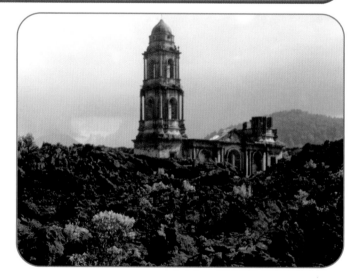

Church spires stick out of the lava field left by the Volcano of Paricutin

FACT FILE

The cone shape of a volcano is made from the ashes and rock that shoot out of it and then compact when they fall back down to the ground.

The Volcano of Paricutin

What makes a volcanic eruption occur

About 60 miles (95 km) under our feet there is a layer of very hot rock that sometimes melts, producing a molten liquid called "magma". Pressure pushes magma towards Earth's surface, where it can "erupt", which means explode violently, through the ground. Magma changes into lava—which is much thicker than magma—and ashes when it is exposed to Earth's atmosphere.

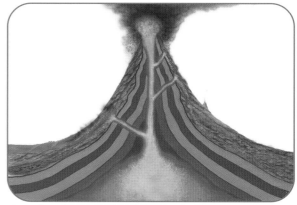

A volcanic eruption

Why is Paricutin so important

Erupting volcanoes had usually existed for thousands of years but, before Paricutin, scientists had never witnessed the actual birth of a volcano. Scientists solved many mysteries surrounding volcanoes by studying Paricutin—such as exactly how magma behaves just before it breaks through Earth's surface.

Where can an active volcano be seen

Mount Etna, in Sicily, is a good place to go. In 2002 and 2003, Etna was the site of one of the most spectacular eruptions of the last four centuries. Some 30 million cubic meters of lava and 40 million cubic meters of rock and ash were produced. Other very active volcanoes include Kilauea in Hawaii and Nyamuragira in Africa.

FACT FILE

The Volcano of Paricutin grew to a height of 1,100 ft (335 m) in just one year and its ash fell on Mexico City, over 200 miles (321 km) away!

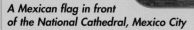

A Mexican flag in front of the National Cathedral, Mexico City

Mount Etna is an active volcano in Sicily

MOUNT EVEREST

Thousands of brave men and women have accepted the ultimate challenge—to climb as high as you can go on Earth and look down from the top of the world!

Where is Mount Everest ❓

Mount Everest is the highest mountain in the world. It is part of the Himalayan range on the borders of Nepal and Tibet. Mount Everest towers above the other

Mount Everest is on the borders of Nepal and Tibet

mountains at 29,029 ft (8,848 m) high. The summit of Mount Everest is as high as you can go on Earth—it really is the top of the world!

FACT FILE

The tectonic plates of India and Asia are still pushing up against each other. As a result of this, Mount Everest grows by 2 in. (5 cm) every year.

Mount Everest, Tibet

How was Mount Everest formed ❓

Roughly sixty million years ago, India, which was then a separate continent on its own tectonic plate, began to move. Eventually, it collided with the "plate" of Asia, and the coasts where the two continents met were pushed up—a bit like the hood of a car in a crash. These coasts became the highest mountain range in the world.

Indian and Asian plates collide

Why is it called Mount Everest

Westerners call it Mount Everest, but the Tibetans call it Chomolungma and the Nepalese call it Sagarmatha—and they should know, because they live at the mountain's base. First recognized as the highest mountain in the world in 1852, it got its Western name ten years later, when Sir George Everest, a British surveyor, came to the area.

Tibetan mother and child

Who were the first men to climb Mount Everest

Climbing Mount Everest has been the ultimate challenge for climbers ever since the 1920s. Climbers have to contend with a lack of oxygen and bitterly cold temperatures. New Zealander Edmund Hillary and his Nepalese guide Sherpa Tenzing Norgay were the first men to successfully reach the summit, on 29th May, 1953.

Sherpa Tenzing Norgay (left) and Edmund Hillary (right)

Who else has climbed Everest

Since 1953, 700 climbers have reached the summit. They have been as young as fifteen and as mature as 64. Junko Tabei became the first woman to reach the top in 1975. The fastest descent came in 1988, when Jean-Marc Boivin paraglided off the summit and reached the base in eleven minutes. Davo Karnicar skied down the mountain in 1980!

Jean-Marc Boivin paraglided off Mount Everest

Mount Everest in the Himalayas

THE COLOSSEUM IN ROME

The design of most modern sports stadiums is based on this truly colossal ancient monument—one of the most famous archaeological wonders of the world.

How big was the Colosseum ?

Until the nineteenth century, the Colosseum in Rome was the largest amphitheatre in the world. It was 165 ft (50 m) high, 600 ft (185 m) long and large enough to hold 50,000 spectators. The façade, or exterior, was three "arcades"—sets of 80 arches—on top of each other. Canvas material was hung from the fourth story to protect spectators from the sun.

ITALY
• Rome

Rome, where the Colosseum ruins can still be found

Why is the Colosseum's design so clever ?

The Colosseum's design is full of "elliptical", or squashed circle, shapes, which allowed more people to fit in. Behind the outer arcades, two corridors circle the building, with two smaller circular corridors inside them. The elliptical arena was surrounded by a wall to protect spectators from wild animals used in the games.

The "elliptical" Colosseum

Who built the Colosseum ?

The Emperor Vespasian began construction in AD 72. His son Titus held the first games there in AD 80, but the building was actually completed by Vespasian's younger son, Domitian, in AD 81. The structure was originally called the Flavian Amphitheatre because all three of these emperors came from a family called Flavius.

Emperor Vespasian

FACT FILE

The Colosseum had 76 vomitoria, which sounds like the sort of place you go to if the games get gruesome. In fact, the word simply means gate!

The Colosseum in Rome

What games were played there

The most popular games were bloody contests between gladiators, or between gladiators and animals. Athletics, battle reenactments and pageants also took place there. Some people think that lions ate Christians in the arena, but this is untrue. Gladiator combat was abolished in AD 404, and the last animal fight was held in AD 523.

A gladiator fighting a tiger

What is the Colosseum like today ?

Fires, earthquakes and neglect have badly damaged the Colosseum since it was last renovated in the early sixth century. However, over one-third of the outer

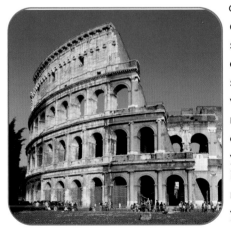

arcades remain and the inner supports for the cavea, or seating space, are also visible. It is in remarkable condition when you consider that it was built nearly 2,000 years ago.

The Colosseum as it looks today

FACT FILE

In films, you often see the Roman Emperor give the "thumbs down" sign when he wants someone killed by a gladiator. In fact, "thumbs up" meant "kill him" and "thumbs down" meant "spare him".

THE GREAT WALL OF CHINA

The largest built structure in the world snakes across deserts, grasslands and mountains—and over two thousand years of history.

How long was the Great Wall of China ❓

The Great Wall once stretched 4,000 miles (6,400 km) from the Korean Peninsula to North-Central China. The Wall had an average height of 32 ft (10 m) and was 16 ft (5 m) wide. Its "snake" shape is due to the fact that it follows the course of the rivers and the contours of the mountains and valleys around it.

The Great Wall of China

CHINA

Extension built during Ming dynasty

FACT FILE

Ordinary people were forced to build the Great Wall. So many of them died that it is sometimes called the "longest cemetery on Earth".

Who built the Great Wall ❓

In the seventh and eighth centuries BC, Chinese rulers built walls to protect their communities. The first emperor, Qin, joined all of these walls together between 221 and 206 BC. Over the next century, the Han emperors extended the Great Wall across the Gobi Desert. The Great Wall was at its longest during the Ming Dynasty of AD 1368 to 1644.

Qin Shi Huang, 1st emperor of China

34

The Great Wall of China stretched 4,000 miles (6,400 km)

Why was the Great Wall built

Ancient China was plagued by attacks from Mongolian and Manchu people. Emperor Qin wanted to build a massive fortification that would stop these raiders from the North. In later centuries, the Great Wall was used to transport soldiers. It was also used to transmit messages across the empire. This was done by burning fires on the watch towers and sending smoke signals.

What state is the Great Wall in

The Great Wall worked for centuries, but after the Manchu seized China in 1644, it fell into disrepair. Even now there are no Chinese laws protecting the Great Wall, although it was made a UNESCO World Heritage Site in 1987. Several hundred miles of the Great Wall remain in Eastern China.

How was the Great Wall built

The early Great Wall was made of earth. During the Ming Dynasty, brick and stone were used to build walls, watch towers and garrison posts. In many areas, there were no farms or towns to provide food, so the workers and the soldiers depended on dangerous mountain supply routes. Many of the builders died.

One of the Great Wall's towers

The Great Wall of China as it stands today

FACT FILE

Some people think that the Great Wall can be seen from space. It can only be seen from a low orbit—as with so many other buildings.

The Great Wall of China seen from a low orbit, TERRA Satellite

THE TAJ MAHAL

One of the most beautiful buildings in the world, the Taj Mahal was built as a monument to love—but it ended up ruining a mighty emperor.

Who were the Mughals ?

The Mughals were fantastically rich Muslim emperors who ruled Northern India from the sixteenth to the nineteenth century AD. They were descended from fearsome Turkish and Mongolian warriors, and early emperors like Akbar, Jehangir and Shahjehan waged war to amass their fortune. The Mughal capital was at Agra, about 124 miles (200 km) south of New Delhi.

Who was the Taj Mahal built for ?

The Mughal Emperor Shahjehan ordered the building of the Taj in 1631, after the death of his wife, Mumtaz Mahal, in childbirth. Shahjehan wanted his wife's tomb to be the most beautiful building in the world. Construction began in 1631 and was completed in 1653. Masons, craftsmen, sculptors, and calligraphers came from all over Asia to work on the masterpiece.

The Mughal Empire (red)

Emperor Shahjehan

Why is the Taj Mahal so beautiful

The Taj is probably the most beautifully proportioned and symmetrical building in the world. It is set in a garden of fountains and ornamental trees. The decoration is very extravagant—some small decorations have fifty gemstones in them. The minarets, or praying towers, have been cleverly designed to make the building look bigger than it really is.

What happened to Shahjehan

It took 22 years and 22,000 workers to complete the Taj Mahal. Shahjehan's memorial was so expensive to build that he had no money left when it was finished. His son deposed him and threw him into prison. From his prison cell Shahjehan could gaze at his wife's tomb through a window.

FACT FILE

When the Taj Mahal was finished, Shahjehan cut his workers' hands off so they couldn't make anything as beautiful ever again.

The famous Indian poet Rabindranath Tagore called the Taj Mahal "a teardrop on the cheek of time".

What is strange about the color of the Taj Mahal

Emperor Shahjehan was so rich that he built the Taj almost completely out of marble. When light strikes the marble at different times of the day or night, it produces different soft colors or hues. In full moonlight, the Taj glows white, at sunrise it looks pink and at sunset it looks gold. Visitors say the effect is very beautiful—and very sad.

The silhouette of the Taj Mahal at dusk

The Taj Mahal, Agra, India

MACHU PICCHU

The lost city of the Inca sits on a remote mountain top in Peru. For nearly four hundred years it lay hidden, with only the roaring river in the valley below to keep it company.

Who were the Inca ?

The Inca Empire was the largest empire in the Americas. It stretched 3,000 miles (4,828 km) from Ecuador to Chile in South America, and had 13 million subjects. The supreme ruler was called the "Inca". The Inca Empire started around AD 1450 and was already ruined by civil war when Spanish invaders arrived in AD 1532.

The Inca Empire (red)

When was Machu Picchu discovered ?

The Spanish didn't believe rumors about a hidden Inca fortress high in the Andes mountains. In 1911, an American, Hiram Bingham, climbed up through a rainforest 120 miles (193 km) from the Inca capital of Cuzco to behold the ruins of a small city. He was the first person to see the city for almost 400 years.

FACT FILE

In modern-day Machu Picchu, llamas are used to keep the grass short!

The impressive city of Machu Picchu

What was Machu Picchu

Machu Picchu (below) is built on terraces on a 9,060-ft (2,761-m) mountain top. It may have been a fortress, a religious center or a royal retreat. Bordered on three sides by precipitous river canyon walls and invisible from below, the people fed themselves by cultivating agricultural terraces. The city had 150 houses, temples and baths.

Why was Machu Picchu abandoned ?

Built in the 1450s, Machu Picchu was mysteriously abandoned just before the Spanish took the Inca capital of Cuzco in 1533. This is probably because the civil war weakened supply lines linking Inca cities, and life at Machu Picchu became too hard. In 1983, UNESCO named Machu Picchu a World Heritage Site and now 500,000 people visit the lost city of the Inca every year.

What is the Intihuatana stone ?

There is an observatory at Machu Picchu. Inside it is an Intihuatana stone—which means "Hitching Post of the Sun" in Quechua, the Inca language. At midday on 21st March and 21st September the

The Intihuatana stone

sun appears directly above this stone and casts no shadow. The Inca believed that at these times they could influence the world around them.

FACT FILE

The building blocks at Machu Picchu weigh 50 tons (45,350 kg) each but fit together so precisely you can't slip a knife blade between them.

TEOTIHUACAN

In the history of mankind, there is only one ancient city that lives up to its name. Teotihuacan really is mysterious and grand enough to be the home of the gods.

Where is Teotihuacan

The city of Teotihuacan was founded 31 miles (50 km) north-east of modern-day Mexico City sometime between AD 100 and AD 200. By the fourth century it was the sixth largest city in the world, stretching for 7 sq miles (20 sq km) and with 200,000 inhabitants. The city was mysteriously burned down and abandoned in AD 750.

Teotihuacan was just north of where Mexico city is today

Who built Teotihuacan

No one knows who built Teotihuacan or lived there. It was named Teotihuacan, which means "the city where the gods were born", by people called the Aztecs—500 years after it was abandoned! The Aztecs believed that only people who were as powerful as gods could have created such enormous pyramids and temples.

Ylaloc, the rain god

What can you see at Teotihuacan

The Pyramid of the Sun is arguably the largest pyramid in the world. It is 207 ft (63 m) high and is built over a sacred cave. This pyramid is connected to the Pyramid of the Moon by the 1¹/₂-mile (2.5-km) Avenue of the Dead. You can also see the amazing Temple of Quetzalcoatl, which is decorated with enormous stone snake heads.

Who was Quetzalcoatl

Quetzalcoatl was the name of both a god and a legendary hero. The god Quetzalcoatl is the god of food, rebirth, butterflies and serpents. He traveled all over Central and South America founding new civilizations. The Aztecs believed that Quetzalcoatl would return at the end of time, which was why they allowed the Spanish conquistadors to destroy them in 1519.

A statue at the temple of Quetzalcoatl

Why is the design of Teotihuacan special

Teotihuacan was the first city in the Americas and its grid structure is still used 1,800 years later! The plan of Teotihuacan is very symmetrical: avenues point north, south, east and west, and the pyramids are modeled on sacred mountains surrounding the city. The city plan resembles butterfly wings—an insect that was sacred to the god Quetzalcoatl.

FACT FILE

The Great Pyramid at Giza is taller than the Pyramid of the Sun but not as large. Another contestant for the world's largest pyramid is the Hotel Luxor in Las Vegas, Nevada (above).

Twice a year the sun sets directly opposite the Pyramid and in a direct line of sight from a long tunnel referred to by archaeologists as "a volcano tube".

The Pyramid of the Sun at Teotihuacan

THE MASAI MARA

In some of the most stunning scenery in the whole of Africa, you can come face to face with the world's wildest animals!

Where is the Masai Mara

The Masai Mara is the most spectacular game reserve in the world. Located south of Kenya's capital, Nairobi, the Masai Mara is part of the great Serengeti plain. It is over 583 sq miles (1,510 sq km) of rolling grassland, rocky outcrops and winding rivers—and boasts one of the highest concentrations of animals and animal species in the world.

Why is the Masai Mara home to so many animals

The region is both humid and fertile. It is crossed by the rivers Mara and Telek, which are full of water all year long. This is unusual in Africa. The river banks are covered in thick bush and lush grassland. The abundance of water and food means there are almost always lions, leopards, cheetahs, elephants, buffalos, zebras, rhinos and hippos to see.

When is the wildebeest migration ?

Migrating wildebeest

Each year, in August and September, millions of animals called wildebeest head to Mara from Serengeti, in search of better grass. This is one of the natural wonders of the world, as the wildebeests move across the plains in 27-mile (44-km) long columns. Predators like lions, leopards, cheetah and hyenas follow the columns, looking for easy prey.

Zebras on the Masai Mara

Who are the Masai

The Masai are a famous warrior tribe whose lives center on the herding of cattle. They live in small settlements called kraals, each of which is made up of between eight and fifteen huts. The kraals are surrounded by a thornbush fence that is sharper than barbed wire. At night, the cattle and other domestic animals are brought inside the kraal for protection.

The Masai Mara in Africa is teeming with wildlife

A Masai tribesman with his cattle

What is a kopje

The rolling plains of the Masai Mara are pitted with rocky outcrops called kopjes. These rocks are millions of years old and home to lions, cheetahs, antelope, mongoose and large Verraux eagles. The kopjes are often decorated with ancient rock paintings, depicting life on the plains. These paintings are made by Masai tribespeople.

A big cat in the wild

FACT FILE

Many people confuse cheetahs (top) and leopards (bottom). The main differences are that a cheetah looks smaller and has a dark "tear mark" running from its eyes to its cheeks.

THE PETRONAS TOWERS

Over the last hundred years or so, people have been trying to construct the tallest building in the world. "Skyscrapers" like these are symbols of pride—but they never hold on to the record for long!

How tall are the Petronas Towers ?

The Petronas Towers in Kuala Lumpur, the capital of Malaysia, are 1,483 ft (452 m) tall. This made them the tallest building in the world at the time of completion. Each of the twin towers has 88 stories, a tapering point and a 242-ft (74-m) spire that brings it to its record-breaking height.

Kuala Lumpur, Malaysia

FACT FILE

The world's tallest man-made structure is the Burj Khalifa, in Dubai which rises to 2,716 ft (828 m), beating the CN tower (shown right) in Toronto, Canada, which stands at 1,815 ft (553 m).

When were the Towers built ?

In 1991, there was an international competition to find a design for the headquarters of the government-owned oil company, Petronas. Architect Cesar Pelli won the competition and building started in 1994. The Petronas Towers cost about $1.6 billion to construct, and opened on 28th August, 1999. The double structure contains a concert hall, a library and an art gallery—as well as offices.

The architect, Cesar Pelli (right)

The Petronas Towers

Why were the Towers built

Skyscrapers are usually built for the "prestige", or honor, they bring their creators. The Petronas Towers were supposed to be a symbol of Malaysia's spectacular economic growth in the 1980s and early 1990s. Many of the Towers' design features also celebrate Malaysia's Muslim culture.

Kek Lok Si Temple, Penang, Malaysia (Malaysian temple)

Unfortunately, a worldwide recession started as building work on the Towers began.

Why are the Towers an architectural marvel

The Petronas Towers have an "arabesque" design and the floor plans are based on the Islamic star. These geometric shapes allow for lots of office space—and great views! The towers are linked by a "skybridge" on the 42nd floor. The exterior is made from ribbons of glass and steel that shimmer in the sun.

The skybridge link

What is the world's tallest building

In October 2003, The 101 tower in Taipei, Taiwan became the world's tallest building. The spire at the top of Taipei 101 makes it 1,666 ft (508 m) high, 183 ft (56 m) taller than the Petronas Towers. The Sears Tower in Chicago still has the highest occupied floor at 1,431 ft (436 m), and the highest roof at 1,454 ft (443 m). In 2010, the Burj Khalifa in Dubai officially opened. It is the tallest man-made structure ever built.

The Taipei 101 Tower (right) and Sears Tower in Chicago (far right)

THE PANAMA CANAL

For centuries, trading nations dreamed of connecting the two great oceans of the world. When they did, it was one of the greatest engineering feats of all time.

What is the Panama Canal ?

The Panama Canal is an 50-mile (81.63-km) waterway through Panama, linking the Atlantic and the Pacific Oceans. Before the canal, ships coming from Europe or the east coast of America traveled 12,958 miles (20,900 km) around South America to get to the west coast. The canal shortened voyages between New York and San Francisco to 5,189 miles (8,370 km).

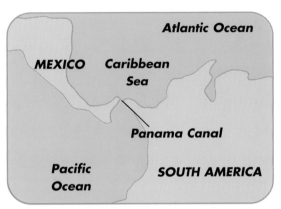

The Panama Canal links two oceans

FACT FILE

Around 12,000 ships make the journey along the Panama Canal each year. The ships are guided by slow-moving, high-powered trains called "mules". As the ships proceed, mules move along each side to guide them in a straight line through the open lock gates.

Who built the Panama Canal ?

In 1534, Charles I of Spain ordered a canal route through the Isthmus of Panama. The French worked on a canal from 1880 to 1900, but disease and financial problems defeated them. In 1903, the US began constructing the canal that is still in use today. Completed in 1914, it cost $387 million!

Charles I Spain

The remarkable engineering feat of the Panama Canal

Why was the Canal such a feat

More than 42,000 people worked for ten years, excavating and dynamiting their way through hard bedrock. They cut through jungles, hills and swamps, and had to deal with tropical diseases like malaria and yellow fever. Engineering feats included building the biggest canal locks in the world and erecting a dam that provided enough power to run the Canal.

Excavation to build the Canal

Why does a canal need locks

Waterways contain height gains called elevations that stop boats from continuing upstream. Canals have an ingenious way of moving boats to, or from, this higher water. Locks use the force of gravity on water to raise and lower boats. In the Panama Canal, one boat uses 52 million gallons of water to move through the Canal's three locks.

Large ships can navigate the Canal

How do canal locks work

A lock has gates at either end. When a ship moves into the lock, the gates close and water is drained out (or pumped in, if the ship wants to go upstream). Due to gravity, the lock's water eventually equals the height of the water downstream or upstream. The gates at the front of the boat are opened and the ship goes on its way.

An illustration of a lock in operation

THE ITAIPU DAM

Find out how a curtain of concrete 738 ft (225 m) high can turn one of the world's greatest rivers into energy and become the world's most powerful dam.

Where is the Itaipu Dam

The Itaipu Dam spans the Parana River on the borders of Brazil and Paraguay in South America. It is a 5-mile (8-km) wide dam, spillway and hydroelectric power plant. The dam is as high as a 65-story building. It was built between 1975 and 1991 and supplies 24 percent of Brazil's energy and 95 percent of Paraguay's.

How does a dam work ?

A dam is a wall built across a river to block the flow of the river. The water builds up behind the dam in a reservoir. Pipes take water from the reservoir to cities, to irrigation projects, or to hydroelectric power stations, as at Itaipu. Here the water passes over turbines—huge wheels attached to motors—to create electricity.

FACT FILE

Other famous dams include the Hoover Dam in America (right), the Aswan Dam in Egypt and the Three Gorges Dam in China—the world's largest.

The Itaipu Hydroelectric Power Plant is the largest in the world.

Hydroelectricity created by water

What is a spillway

The pressure of the water behind a dam can damage its structure, so every dam has a spillway. This works just like the overflow of a bath. When the water reaches a certain level, usually during floods, it flows down the spillway and back into the river below the dam. Itaipu's spillway can discharge 62,200 cubic meters of water per second.

A dam's spillway

How powerful is the Itaipu Dam

Itaipu's powerhouse, where electricity is created, contains eighteen hydroelectric generators, each of them 53 ft (16 m) wide. Some 165 tons of water per second pour onto each turbine, generating 12,600 MW (megawatts) of electricity. The power plant's eighteen generating units have a total production capacity of 12,600 MW and a record-breaking output of eighty million MW a year.

Why do dams affect the environment

The creation of a reservoir means flooding the area behind the dam, which can destroy the delicate balance of an area's ecology. When Egypt's Aswan Dam was made, the builders had to move lots of ancient monuments. The Chinese government had to rehouse over one million people when they built the Three Gorges Dam.

The Aswan Dam

THE EMPIRE STATE BUILDING

The most famous skyscraper in the world was the tallest building for over forty years. It remains the standard against which all other skyscrapers are judged.

What was the skyscraper race ?

The skyscraper race began with the Eiffel Tower (984 ft/299 m), in Paris in 1889. American architects, competing among themselves, started to build ever-taller buildings: the Metropolitan Life Tower of 1909 (700 ft/213 m); the Woolworth Building of 1913 (792 ft/241 m); 1929's Bank of Manhattan Building (927 ft/282 m); and the Chrysler Building in 1930 (1,046 ft/318 m).

The towers involved in the skyscraper race

When was the Empire State Building built ?

Construction began in 1930 and was completed just one year and 45 days later, in May 1931. The Empire State Building is 1,250 ft (381 m) high and remained the tallest building in the world until the completion of the World Trade Center in 1972. Tragically, the World Trade Center was destroyed by terrorists in 2001.

World Trade Center (far left)

There are 1,575 steps inside the Empire State Building. In 2001, Paul Crake set the record for running up to the top—he did it in 10 minutes 15 seconds.

Using the elevators, it is possible to travel to the 80th floor of the Empire State Building in 45 seconds.

The Empire State Building

How was the Empire State Building built so fast

Workers known as skywalkers put up the immense frame, weighing over 55,116 tons in just 23 weeks. Passersby would gaze up at them as they worked hundreds of feet above the ground, walking along the girders they put in place the day before to hammer big nails called rivets into steel girders higher up the structure.

A "skywalker" at work

What was the Empire State Building going to be used for

In the early 1930s, the skyscraper was going to be an airport for dirigibles (also known as zeppelins or blimps) which were to be moored on the 102nd floor observation deck. The Observation Lounge that you can still visit on the 86th floor was going to be the departure lounge.

The damaged building after the plane crash

What happened to Betty Lou Oliver

On 28th September, 1945, Betty Lou Oliver was working as an elevator operator in the Empire State Building, when a B-25 bomber crashed into it. The bomber's left engine sliced through the elevator's cables and Betty Lou rocketed over 1,000 ft (300 m) down the shaft in just seven seconds. The elevator ended up in a cellar, but luckily Betty Lou survived.

THE GOLDEN GATE BRIDGE

People said this magnificent bridge couldn't be built, but for sixty years after its completion, the Golden Gate Bridge was the world's tallest suspension bridge.

What is a suspension bridge ?

A suspension bridge has a deck (the bit pedestrians and motorists use) that is suspended from cables. The cables pass over

Head on view of suspension bridge

towers and are secured in the earth. Bridges are subject to compression, a force that pushes down on the deck. The cables transfer this force to the towers from where it runs into the earth. Another force, called tension, affects the cables, but they are made taut and safe by the weight of the bridge.

FACT FILE

The construction of the Golden Gate Bridge was the first time protective hard hats were worn on building sites.

The Golden Gate Bridge contains enough cable to go around Earth three times!

How big is the Golden Gate Bridge ?

The bridge spans 1¹/₄ miles (1.93 km) and can sway up to 27 ft (8.2 m) to withstand 100 mph (160 km/h) winds. The two towers are 746 ft (227 m) high and the cables—the biggest ever to support a bridge—are 361 ft (110 m) thick. Work on the bridge began on 5th January 1933, ended on 27th May, 1937, and cost $35 million.

Thick cables support the bridge

The Golden Gate Bridge

In 1847, thousands of people came to San Francisco to look for gold in the Californian Gold Rush. The entrance to San Francisco Bay became known as the Golden Strait (or narrow channel). The Golden Gate Bridge spans this strait and was named after it.

Why was it thought impossible to build ?

The Golden Gate Bridge was considered impossible to build because of the fog, winds and ocean currents in the Bay. Workers wore goggles, hand cream and face cream—and a safety net was strung under the Bridge to protect them. They were also given special food so they wouldn't get dizzy!

A brave worker paints the Bridge

61

GLOSSARY

Agra
A city in north India and capital of the Mogul empire until 1658.

Alexandria
The chief port of Egypt on the Nile Delta: cultural center of ancient times, founded by Alexander the Great.

Amazons
One of a race of women warriors of Scythia near the Black Sea.

Artemis
An ancient Greek goddess who was the twin sister of Apollo.

Asia Minor
The historical name for Anatolia (the Asian part of Turkey).

Auroras
An atmospheric phenomenon consisting of bands, curtains, or streamers of light, that move across the sky. As in aurora borealis (Northern Lights) and aurura australis (Southern Lights).

Babylon
The chief city of the ancient Mesopotamia. Home of the Hanging Gardens of Babylon.

Canyon
A gorge or ravine, especially in North America, usually formed by a river.

Chomolungma
The Tibetan name for Mount Everest, the highest mountain in the world.

Colosseum
An amphitheatre in Rome built around AD 75–80.

Colossus
A structure that's very large, such as a statue.

Conquistador
An adventurer or conqueror, especially one of the Spanish conquerors of the New World in the 16th century.

Crusader
European Christians who fought with Muslims to capture the Holy Land.

Cuzco
A city in south-central Peru: former capital of the Inca Empire, with extensive Inca remains.

Dam
A barrier of concrete, earth etc, built across a river to create a contained body of water.

Dirigible
Another name for an airship or a blimp.

Ecology
The study of the relationships between living organisms and their environment.

Emperor
A male monarch who rules or reigns over an empire.

Erosion
The wearing away of rocks and soil, etc, by the action of water, wind, ice etc.

Giza (El Giza)
A city in north-east Egypt, on the west bank of the Nile opposite Cairo.

Gladiator
A man trained to fight in arenas to provide entertainment.

Gold Rush
Started in 1848. More than 90,000 people made their way to California in the two years following James Marshall's discovery, and more than 300,000 by 1854.

Goth
A member of the East Germanic people from Scandinavia who settled south of the Baltic early in the first millennium.

Halicarnassus
A major Greek colony of the south coast of Asia Minor.

Helios
The ancient Greek god of the sun, who drove his chariot daily across the sky.

Hippolyte
A queen of the Amazons, slain by Hercules in a battle for her belt.

GLOSSARY

Inca
A member of the South American Indian people whose empire, centered on Peru, lasted from about AD 1100 to the Spanish Conquest in the early 1530s.

Kopje
A small, isolated hill.

Khufu
An ancient Egyptian king who was buried in the Great Pyramid.

Lava
Lava flowing from a volcano.

Magma
The molten liquid that results when a layer of very hot rock under the ground melts.

Machu Picchu
A ruined Inca city in south central Peru.

Manchu
A person from Manchuria, north-east China.

Masai
A member of a Nilotic people, formerly noted as warriors, living chiefly in Kenya and Tanzania.

Mausoleum
A large, stately tomb.

Ming Dynasty
The Imperial Dynasty of China from 1368 to 1644.

Mongolian
An inhabitant of Mongolia, central Asia.

Muslim
A follower of the religion of Islam.

Olympians
Of, or relating to, Mount Olympus or the classical Greek gods.

Paricutin
A volcano in west central Mexico, in Michoacan state, formed in 1943 after a week of Earth tremors.

Pharaoh
The title of the ancient Egyptian kings.

Pharos
Any marine lighthouse or beacon.

Plateau
A wide, mainly flat area of elevated land.

Pyramid
A huge masonry construction that has a square base and four sloping, triangular sides.

Rhodes
A Greek Island in the south-east Aegean Sea, about 10 miles (16 km) off the Turkish coast.

Roman
Of, or relating to, Rome or its inhabitants in ancient or modern times.

Satrap
A governor in ancient Persia.

Serengeti
A park that covers 5,700 sq miles (14,763 sq km) of rolling plains in the African country of Tanzania.

Sidon
The chief city of ancient Phoenicia founded in the third millennium BC.

Skyscraper
A very tall multi-story building.

Solar
Of, or relating to, the sun.

Summit
The highest part of a mountain.

Taj Mahal
A marble mausoleum in central India, in Agra: built (1632–53) by the emperor Shahjehan in memory of his wife.

Tectonic Plates
These are the results of the distortion of Earth's crust due to forces within it.

Trilobite
An extinct type of Marine creature.

UNESCO
United Nations Educational, Scientific, and Cultural Organisation.

Vomitoria
A passageway that opens to a tier of seats.

Zeus
The supreme god of the ancient Greeks. The ruler of gods and men.

INDEX